DRAGONS

Contents

Diana Bentley
and Sylvia Karavis

Story illustrated by
Tom Percival

Before Reading

Find out about

- Lots of different lizards and what they are like

Tricky words

- dragon
- breathe
- fire
- people
- lizard
- fierce

Introduce these tricky words and help the reader when they come across them later!

Text starter

In films and books, dragons are fierce, flying creatures with huge wings and a long tail. They breathe fire and sometimes eat people! There are no dragons in the real world – but some lizards are a bit like dragons!

Today's Dragons

This is a dragon in a film.

- It has a long tail.
- It can fly.
- It can breathe fire.
- It can eat people!

This Common Lizard has a long tail. Do you think it looks like a dragon?

Is the Common Lizard like a dragon?

The Common Lizard looks a bit like a dragon. But ...
- It cannot fly.
- It cannot breathe fire.
- It cannot eat people!

This lizard is called an Iguana. It has long claws and looks really fierce.

Do you think the Iguana looks like a dragon?

The Iguana looks a bit
like a dragon. But ...
- It cannot fly.
- It cannot breathe fire.
- It cannot eat people!

This is a Flying Lizard.
It has wings.
It cannot fly, but it can glide.

The Flying Lizard looks a bit like a dragon. But ...
- It cannot breathe fire.
- It cannot eat people!

These Komodo Dragons are the biggest lizards in the world. They cannot fly. They cannot breathe fire.

But ...

- They are really fierce.
- They CAN eat people!

Quiz

Text Detective

- What is the one thing that only a dragon can do?
- Which lizard do you think is most like a dragon?

Word Detective

- **Phonic Focus: Blending three phonemes**
  Page 5: Sound out 'bit' and 'but'. What is different?
- Page 8: Find a word which is the opposite of 'can'.
- Page 10: Why is the word 'CAN' in capital letters?

Super Speller

Read these words:

fly   this   looks

Now try to spell them!

HA! HA! HA!

Q What are the best steps to take if you see a man-eating dragon?

A Very long ones.

In this story

 Sir Bold

 Hal

 The dragon

 Flash

Tricky words

- notice
- dragon
- reward
- lance
- sword
- rope

Introduce these tricky words and help the reader when they come across them later!

Story starter

Sir Bold was a poor knight who lived long ago. He had a faithful servant called Hal and an old horse called Flash. One day Sir Bold saw a notice offering a reward for capturing a fierce dragon.

Sir Bold and the Dragon

Sir Bold read the notice. "I will get the dragon," said Sir Bold. "Then I will get the reward."

Sir Bold and Hal saw a path. "The dragon went this way," said Sir Bold.

"No," said Hal. "It went this way."

They saw a lake.
"The dragon went this way,"
said Sir Bold.

"No," said Hal. "It went
this way."

Who do you think is right –
Sir Bold or Hal?

15

They came to a cave.
The dragon was sleeping
in the cave.

"I have an idea," said Sir Bold.
"I will get the dragon with
my lance – but you go first."

"I have an idea," said Sir Bold. "I will get the dragon with my sword – but you go first."

Why does Sir Bold want Hal to go first?

"I have an idea," said Hal. "I will get the dragon with my rope."

"Here is the dragon," said Hal.

Sir Bold and Hal took the dragon to the town.

"I got the dragon," said Sir Bold.

"No you didn't!" said the dragon.
"It was Hal!"

So Hal got the reward.

Quiz

Text Detective

- How can you tell Sir Bold is not very brave?
- Who do you think deserved the reward?

Word Detective

- **Phonic Focus:** Blending three phonemes
  Page 19 and 21: Sound out 'get' and 'got'.
  What is different?
- Page 15: Find a word which rhymes with 'make'
- Page 23: Find a word meaning 'prize'.

Super Speller

Read these words:

read   with   didn't

Now try to spell them!

HA! HA! HA!

Q When are dragons most likely to eat you?

A On Chewsday.

24